St. James
Catholic School
Montague, Michigan

SCIENCE IN ACTION
The Forces with You!

By Tom Johnston
Illustrated by Sarah Pooley

Gareth Stevens Publishing
Milwaukee

St. James
Catholic School
Montague, Michigan

Library of Congress Cataloging-in-Publication Data

Johnston, Tom.
　　The forces with you!

　(Science in action)
　　Originally published: Let's imagine forces: London: The Bodley Head.
　　Includes index.
　　Summary: Explains how forces such as gravity, friction, elasticity, and inertia and agents of force such as leverage and balance affect our lives.
　　1. Force and energy--Juvenile literature. (1. Force and energy)
I. Pooley, Sarah, ill. II. Title. III. Series: Science in action (Milwaukee, Wis.)
QC73.4.J64　1988　　　531　　　87-42753
ISBN 1-55532-408-8 (lib. bdg.)
ISBN 1-55532-433-9 (trade bdg.)

North American edition first published in 1988 by

Gareth Stevens, Inc.　7317 West Green Tree Road
Milwaukee, Wisconsin 53223, USA

This US edition copyright © 1988. First published as *Let's Imagine: Forces* in the United Kingdom by
The Bodley Head, London.

Text copyright © 1985 Tom Johnston
Illustrations copyright © 1985 Sarah Pooley
Additonal artwork copyright © 1988 Gareth Stevens, Inc.

All rights reserved. No part of this book may be reproduced or utilized in any form or by any means
without permission in writing from Gareth Stevens, Inc.

Hand lettering: Kathy Hall
Additional artwork on page 31: Sheri Gibbs
Typeset by Web Tech, Milwaukee
Project editor: Mark Sachner

Technical consultants: Jonathan Knopp, Chair, Science Department, Rufus King High School, Milwaukee;
Willette Knopp, Reading Specialist and Elementary Teacher, Fox Point-Bayside (Wis.) School District.

2 3 4 5 6 7 8 9 93 92 91 90 89 88

Of all the forces that affect us, gravity is probably the one we notice most. We often call this force by another name — weight. Gravity and weight are the same thing. The more massive a thing is, the more gravity pulls on it, and so the heavier it feels.

It was the famous scientist Isaac Newton who found out most of the things we now know about gravity. In 1687 he published his theories (ideas) in a book called *Principia Mathematica*. In this he explained that it is the Earth's gravity which makes things fall. He also suggested the more surprising idea that every object, however small, attracts every other object gravitationally. This attraction between small things, like you and this book, is so weak a force that you don't notice it.

We now measure force in units known as newtons (named after Sir Isaac). In everyday use, we measure weight in pounds or kilograms, but this is wrong scientifically. Your mass (everything you are made of) should be calculated in pounds or kilograms, but your weight is a force and should be measured in newtons.

A story is told of how Isaac Newton was once sitting under a tree when an apple fell on his head. He realized that the Earth's gravity pulled the apple toward it, and this made him think about the forces that kept the moon moving around the Earth.

If you were to fly to the moon, some strange things would happen. Wherever you go your mass always stays the same, but your weight can change. As you left the Earth's gravity behind, you would become nearly weightless (weigh nothing), but since there is still the same amount of you, your mass would remain unchanged. As you came closer to the moon, you would begin to feel its gravity pulling on you, so you would gain a little weight. Having landed, you would weigh only one-sixth of your normal Earth weight, because, as a smaller body, the moon has gravity that is only one-sixth that of Earth's.

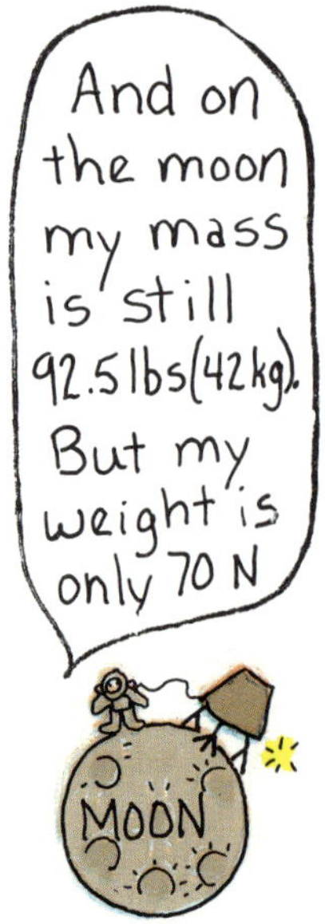

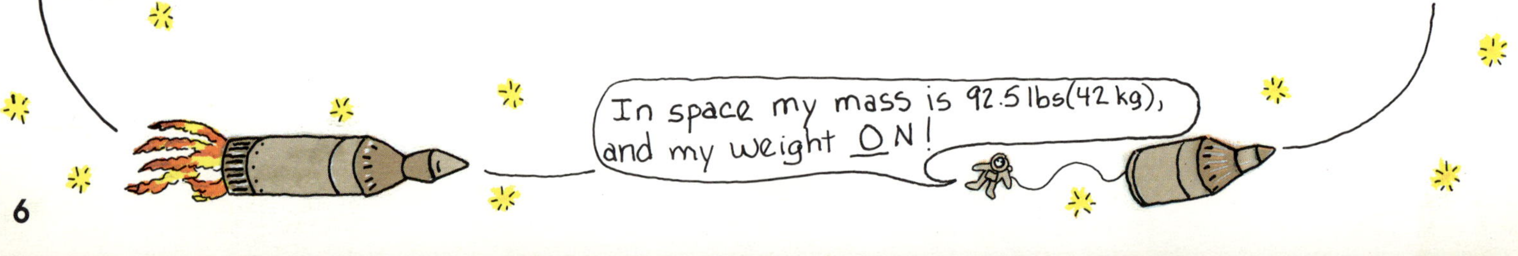

"A discus thrower uses this effect when she spins around before letting the discus go!"

"And so does a hammer thrower!"

The sun's gravity pulls on all the planets in the solar system, in the same way as the Earth's gravity pulls on the moon. Because the planets are moving very quickly through space, they don't crash into the sun.

Try this experiment:

Stand outside, well away from any windows, and above your head spin an object like a glove or a plastic bracelet on the end of a long piece of string. Let it go. You will see it fly off in an almost straight line. The force of your hand has been pulling inward along the string, keeping the object moving in a circle. In the same way the sun's gravity holds the planets in orbit around it. Without the sun, planets would fly off in straight lines.

"Let's get out of here!"

"A dryer uses this effect, too. It spins the laundry around, but the water flies off in straight lines through the holes in the drum."

"Here goes..."

— COME ON ANITA!

"Stop talking about spin-dryers and concentrate on Anita "Who-Can-Beat-Her" Jones!"

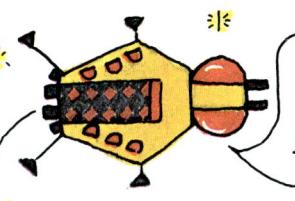
"Intergalactica to mission control. Bleep. Ultimate speed reached. Switch off rockets."

"Bleep. Going in to land on alien territory. Bleep."

Here is another way to show this force:

Set up your experiment. Hold the cardboard tube high above your head and spin the keys. Like magic, the water-filled bottle will rise off the ground.

Spin the keys faster. What happens?

The bottle rises higher.

Spin the keys slower. Now what happens?

The bottle falls.

As the small mass spins faster, it moves outward, pulling the larger mass up. The small mass is trying to move outward in a straight line, but the force of gravity on the larger mass pulls it inward.

In fact, without forces, like gravity, to stop them from moving, objects would keep going in a straight line forever. This effect will be very important if humans ever build intergalactic spacecraft. A vehicle on Earth needs to use fuel all the time to keep going. But a spacecraft could switch off its rockets once it had gone beyond the pull of the sun's gravity and reached the necessary speed. It would then keep going at that speed and in a straight line without slowing down.

"Mission control. Proceeding to destination. Bleep. Reaching required speed. Bleep."

"Switch on engine. Bleep. Full power. Bleep. No sign of human life or other life. Bleep. Over and out."

Of course, gravity isn't the only force that affects things. A car's engine produces the force to keep it going. A heavy vehicle, like a truck, needs more force to start it moving (or to speed it up) than a small car would. The truck also needs more force to stop, so it must have stronger brakes.

We say that hard-to-move objects have lots of inertia. Lighter objects have less inertia.

If you live near some swings, you can try out this experiment. It will show you how your own inertia works:

| GET SWINGING! (But not <u>too</u> high!) | JUMP OFF! | NOW TRY TO STAND STILL! |

When you jump off the swing, you have to run or fall forward. Once your body is moving forward, your inertia makes it difficult for you to stop or go in another direction. Probably you have felt the same effect in a bus or a car when it brakes suddenly. The bus stops, but you keep going forward.

Even if you were firmly strapped into a car and blindfolded, you would still be able to sense if it had braked sharply. Inside your ear, and separate from your hearing system, you have an "inertial" sensing system. We sometimes refer to this as our "sense of balance." It uses an inertial effect to make it work.

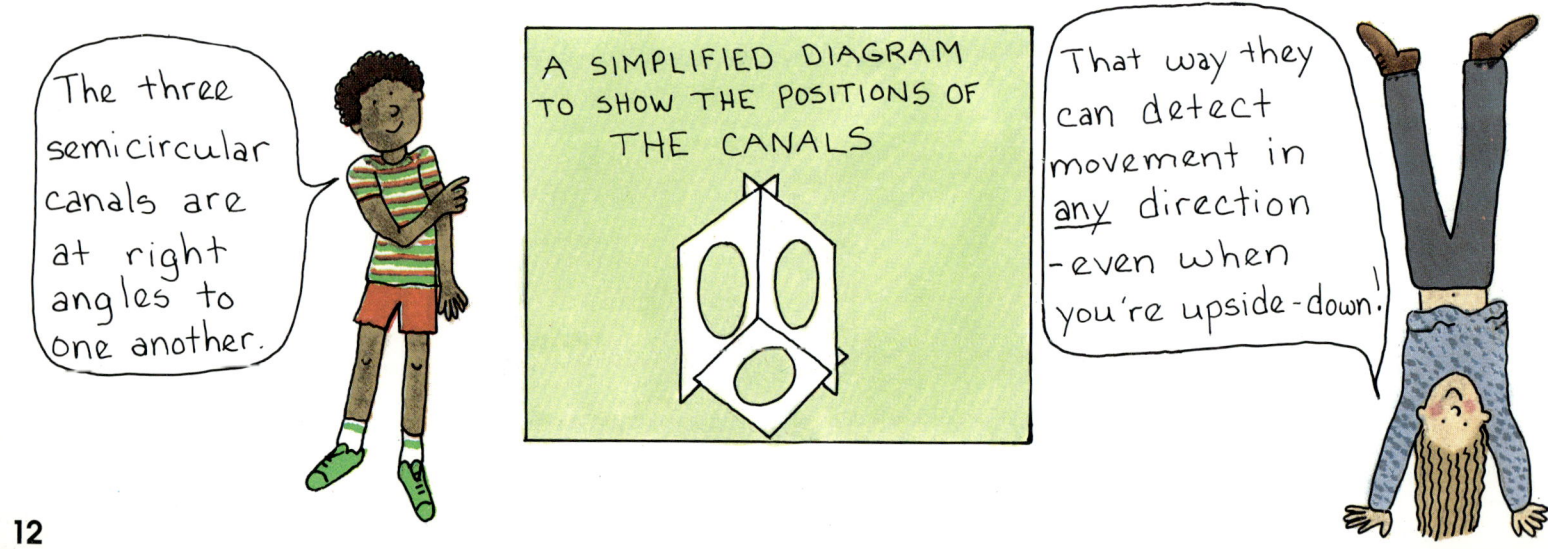

"Can you imagine doing these sports without inertia? Just look..."

① A pole vaulter wouldn't be able to vault far!

② A Judo Dan wouldn't be able to throw her opponent!

③ A javelin thrower's javelin wouldn't break any records!

Kind of like the jar of water, your ear has three fluid-filled tubes, called semicircular canals. As your head or body moves, the fluid in these tubes lags behind, and nerves in your ear can detect this.

"The three semicircular canals are at right angles to one another."

A SIMPLIFIED DIAGRAM TO SHOW THE POSITIONS OF THE CANALS

"That way they can detect movement in any direction - even when you're upside-down!"

If we want to get something moving, we must overcome not only inertia but also another important force — friction.

You can feel one effect of friction if you rub your hands together. If you rub them together quickly, they can get very hot.

Friction seems to be caused by atoms of materials "sticking" together where they touch. Atoms are the tiny parts that all things are made from.

Another important force affecting all our lives is the elastic force. Elastic force is involved when something is stretched or squashed and then springs back to shape again. The elastic force of a spring keeps a wound-up clock ticking, and the elastic force of a rubber band fires a slingshot. You can use the elastic force of a rubber band to make this moving model. The wound-up rubber band produces the force to drive the "car" along.

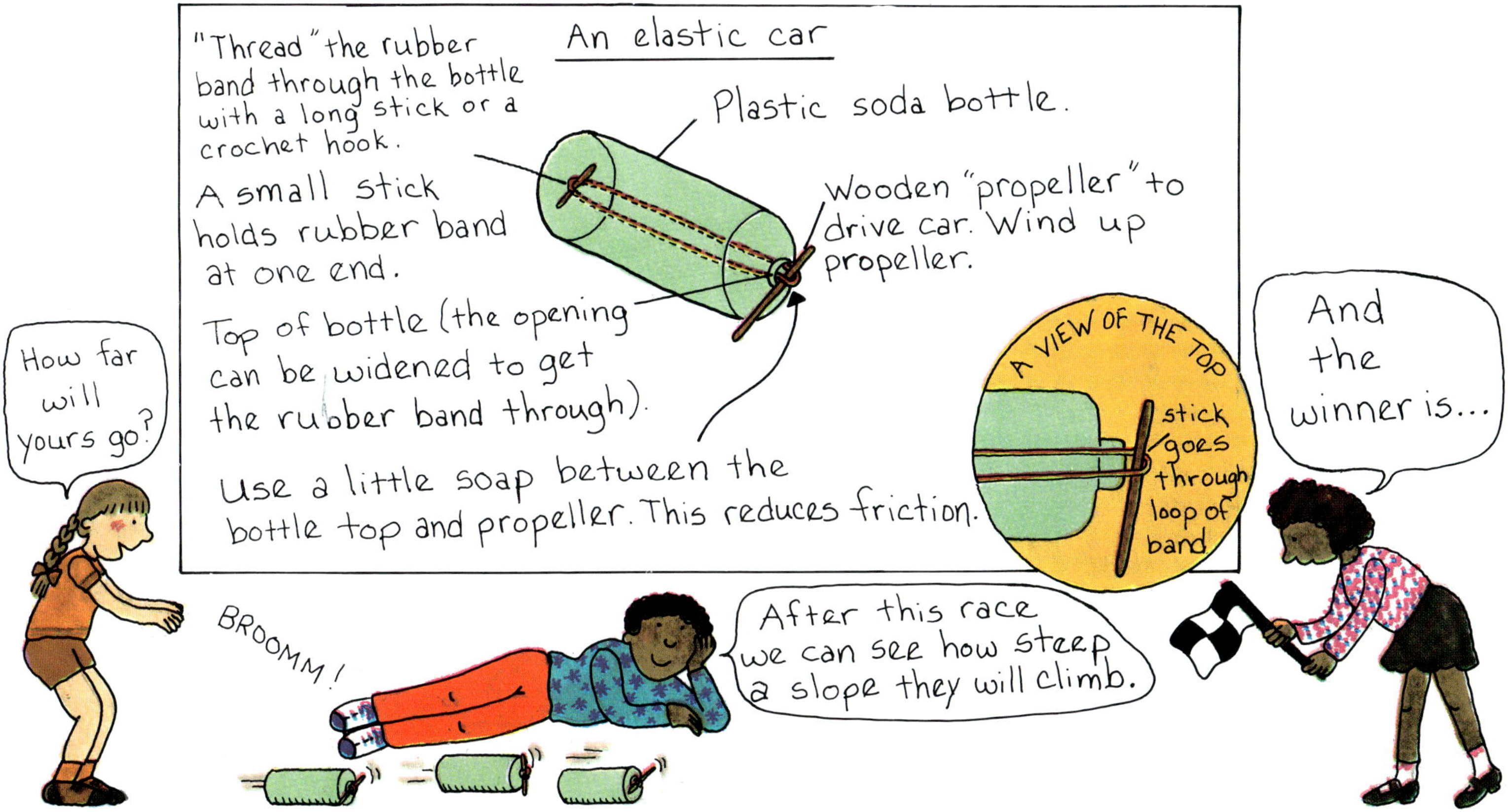

An elastic car

"Thread" the rubber band through the bottle with a long stick or a crochet hook.

A small stick holds rubber band at one end.

Plastic soda bottle.

Wooden "propeller" to drive car. Wind up propeller.

Top of bottle (the opening can be widened to get the rubber band through).

Use a little soap between the bottle top and propeller. This reduces friction.

A VIEW OF THE TOP — stick goes through loop of band

How far will yours go?

BROOMM!

After this race we can see how steep a slope they will climb.

And the winner is...

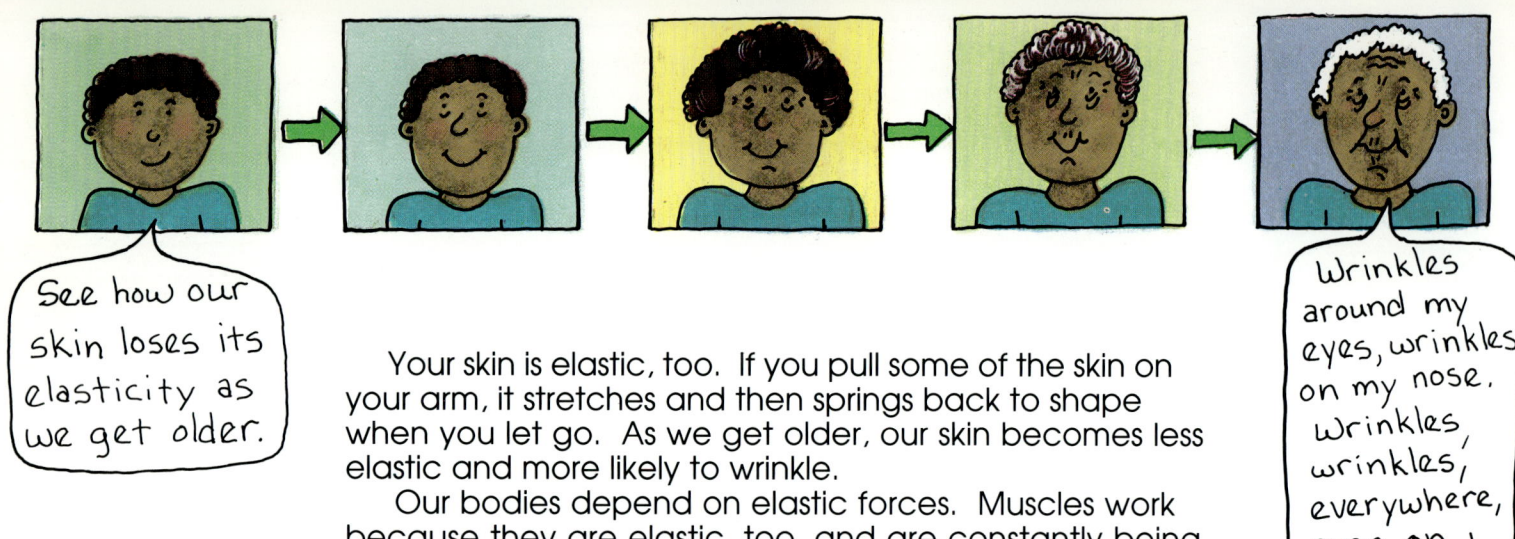

"See how our skin loses its elasticity as we get older."

"Wrinkles around my eyes, wrinkles on my nose. Wrinkles, wrinkles, everywhere, even on my toes!"

Your skin is elastic, too. If you pull some of the skin on your arm, it stretches and then springs back to shape when you let go. As we get older, our skin becomes less elastic and more likely to wrinkle.

Our bodies depend on elastic forces. Muscles work because they are elastic, too, and are constantly being contracted and relaxed. They are made of tiny fibers, each of which has its own nerve. These nerves tell the fibers when to contract. This makes the whole muscle shorter and produces a pulling force. To produce more force, the nerves make more fibers pull.

"Switching on the television uses muscle power... phew! But cleaning up my room would use a lot more!"

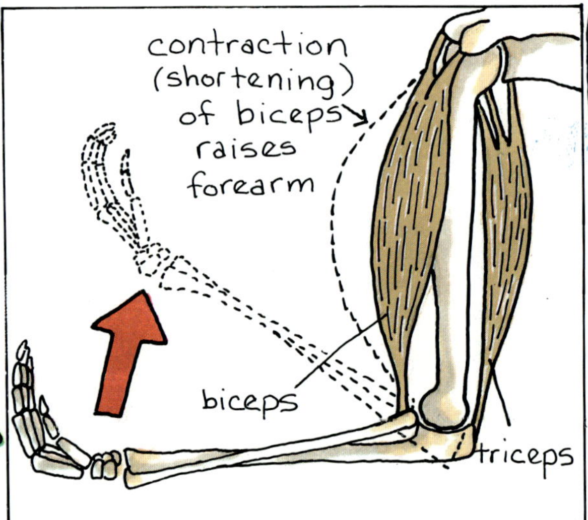

contraction (shortening) of biceps raises forearm

biceps

triceps

MUSCLES OF THE FOREARM

"Weightlessness in space makes muscles weak, so astronauts must exercise to keep themselves fit."

Unlike an elastic band, your muscles can get tired. This is because to produce a force the fibers have to keep being told to contract by the nerves. The faster the fibers contract, the more force they produce.

Human muscle can produce enough force to break a brick in half. The force of an Olympic sprinter's muscles can propel him or her at about 22 miles (35 km) per hour.

Our muscles use forces in a special way. They are attached to our bones, and together they make a system of levers. A lever is a simple machine, and machines are really just ways of making forces work for us more usefully.

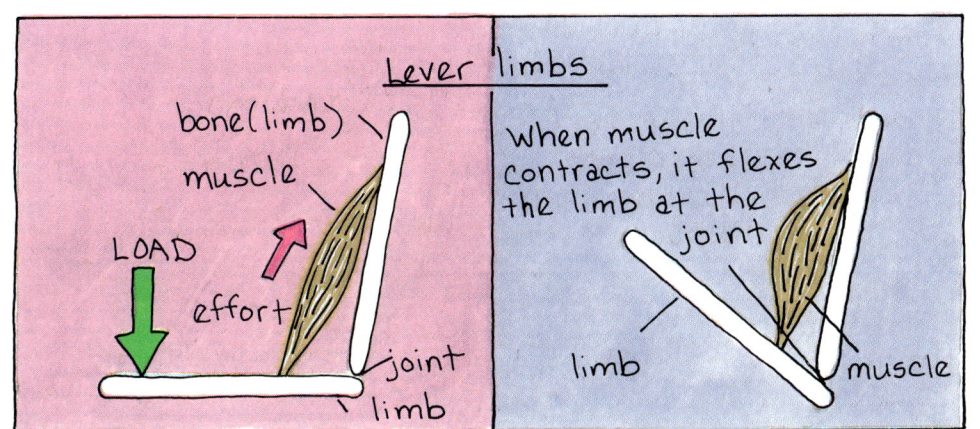

If you have several pairs of differently shaped scissors, find out which ones are best at cutting through thick pieces of cardboard. You should find that the scissors with the longest handles and shortest blades are the best. The reason for this is explained in this way:

If the distance on her side of the pivot is long enough, the girl can move a large force with only a little effort.

If the distance on her side of the pivot is short, the girl will have to make a large effort to move only a small force.

A playground seesaw is also a lever. Here, we keep the forces on both sides more or less balanced, adding a little extra force (foot-pushing) to make it move up and down.

Some scales weigh things by balancing forces. You put the object you want to weigh on one side of the pivot and the weights on the other side until the balance is level.

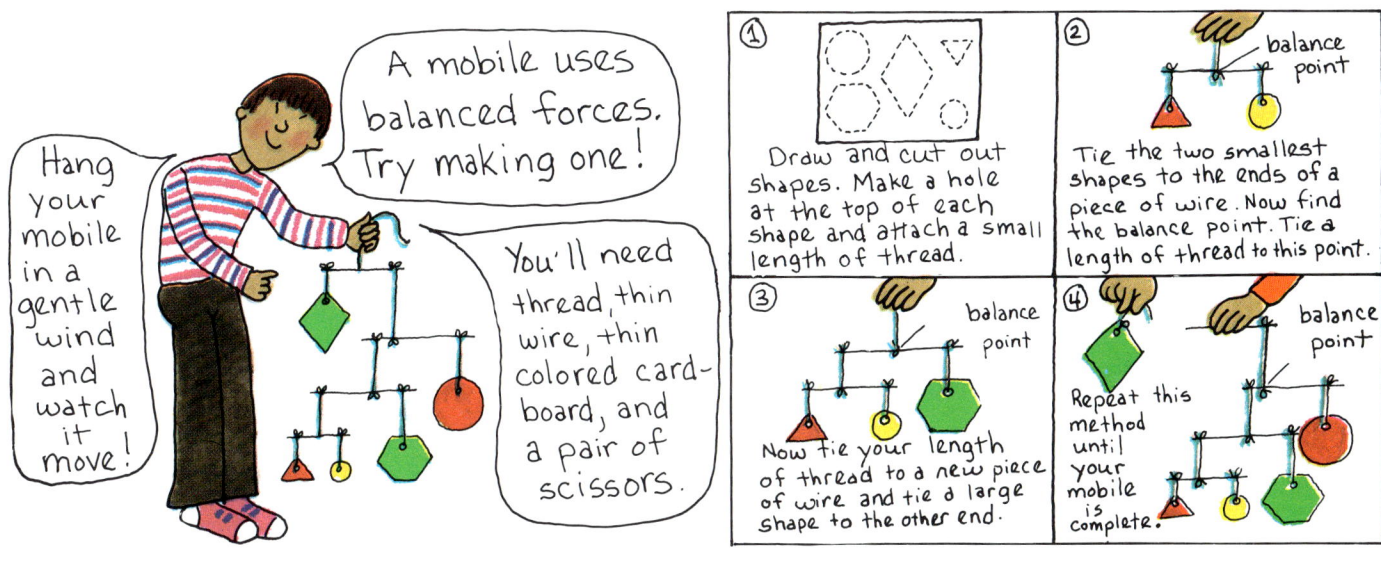

This center of gravity is important for balancing. You can use your own body to show this. Your center of gravity is roughly in the middle of your chest. When you are standing upright, your center of gravity is above your feet. If it were not, you would fall over.

> Lean up against a wall sideways so that your head, shoulder, hip, and ankle touch the wall on your left. Keep your feet together. Now lift your right foot.

> Oooh! You'll fall over!

> Try again with your back to the wall. Your head and heels should be touching it. See if you can bend forward to touch your toes. Once more you will fall over!

We use this same principle to make objects more stable. Tall buses have a low center of gravity so they will not tip over easily. Long wine bottles have a wide, heavy base — also to keep their center of gravity low.

"There are two stories about how magnets were discovered and named. The first tells of a Greek boy, Magnes, who was out tending his sheep when his iron staff stuck to a rock! The rock was named after him!"

"The other story tells of magnetic rock being found near the city of Magnesia in Asia Minor. The modern name for magnetic iron ore is magnetite. Which story do you believe?"

Of all the forces, probably the strangest are the magnetic ones. You probably at some time have played with two magnets and "felt" the forces between them. The ends of a magnet, where the magnetism seems to be, are called its poles. If you allow a magnet to swing freely, the end that points north is called the north pole of the magnet. If you bring two north poles together, they push apart. But if you put a north and south pole together, they attract each other.

MAKE YOUR OWN COMPASS - IT'S EASY!

① First make a permanent magnet out of a sewing needle. Do this by stroking a needle, in one direction only, on a magnet.

② Take your magnetized needle and place it on a cork. Float the cork in a bowl full of water. The North pole of the needle points northwards and the South pole points southwards.

You have probably also used a plastic comb, rubbed on your hair or clothes, to pick up small pieces of paper. If not, try it now! This effect is sometimes called static electricity.

TRY THE SAME EFFECT WITH BALLOONS!

23

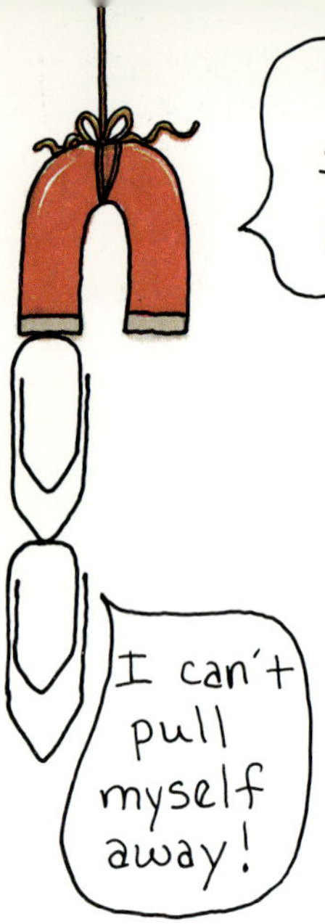

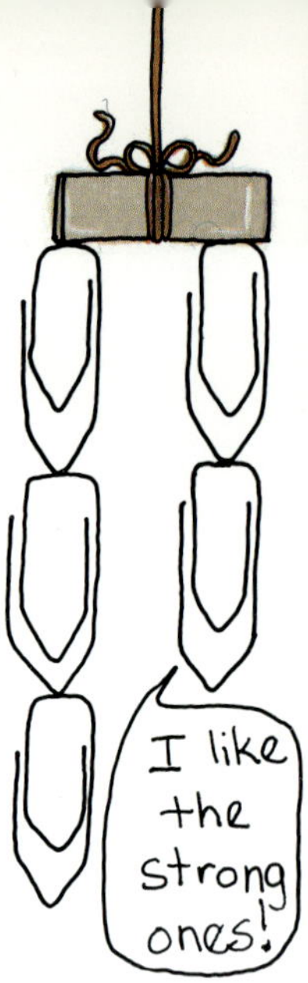

"Hey! These paper clips seem to like my *magnetic* personality!"

"They seem to find me even *more* attractive!"

"I can't pull myself away!"

"I like the strong ones!"

Both the magnetic and the electrical forces have common effects: they can attract (pull) or repel (push) things.

Neither electrical nor magnetic forces are very strong. You can compare the strength of different magnets by seeing how many paper clips they will pick up. The strength of the static electrical force can be measured using an electroscope made from a glass jar, a piece of copper wire, and a strip of thin aluminum foil.

"Hold a comb that has been rubbed with a cloth in this position. The sides of the foil will move apart! Now try some other plastic objects."

"Rub each piece of plastic on a cotton cloth and then hold it near the top of the copper wire. See how far apart the sides of the aluminum strip move."

After you've tested one piece of plastic, touch the top of the wire with your hand. This will make the strips move together again. We call this "discharging." The plastic that causes most movement is producing the biggest electrical force.

How does this force work? In rubbing the plastic, the friction "charges" it. This electrical charge is then passed through the copper wire to the aluminum strip. The two charged sides of the strip push each other apart, just as similar magnetic poles repel each other. Just as there are two types of magnetic pole, north and south, so there are two types of electrical charge, positive (+) and negative (-).

Although natural magnetic and electrical forces are small, larger man-made magnetic forces can be produced by an electric current. This larger force is called an electromagnetic force.

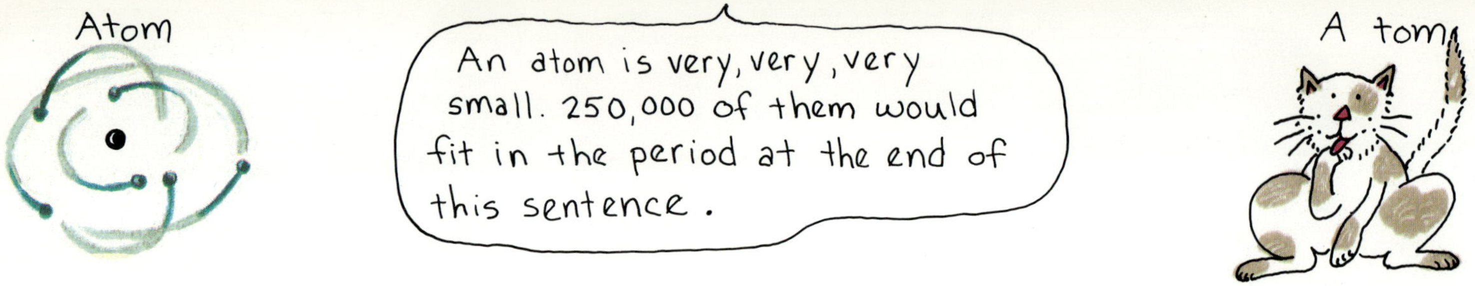

Atom

A tom

An atom is very, very, very small. 250,000 of them would fit in the period at the end of this sentence.

Earlier we mentioned atoms — the tiny parts from which all things are made. Well, atoms are made of even smaller particles that are electrically charged. Each atom has an equal number of positively charged particles (protons) and negatively charged particles (electrons). Protons and electrons attract each other, so we say that the atom is neutral (has no overall charge). Sometimes, however, atoms lose negative charges to become positive overall, or gain negative charges to become negative overall. We call these charged atoms ions. Many common things are held together by the attracting force between positive and negative ions.

This is how atoms join together in common table salt. The chemical name for salt is sodium chloride.

Salt is made from positive sodium ions and negative chlorine ions. They join together by attracting each other.

This is how scientists write salt. It's in shorthand!

Sodium Chloride

So we put ions on our fries!

Scientists believe that it is the electrical forces between atoms that explain friction and elastic forces. In fact, all the other forces, except gravity, are caused by the electrical forces between atoms.

Of course, scientists do not know everything about forces, and today many scientists are trying to discover which forces hold the universe together. They are looking at all the different forces and trying to find a theory that will link all the forces together. They think there are four basic forces in nature: gravity (which is the weakest), electromagnetic force, and two they call the "weak" and "strong" forces. These last two forces act inside the tiny particles that atoms are made of. Exciting new developments are taking place that may change the way scientists think about forces and, indeed, about the whole universe.

Scientists investigating how the universe is held together...

One bridge that didn't stand up to high winds was the Tay Bridge in Scotland. It fell down during a storm in 1879, bringing a train with it and killing many people.

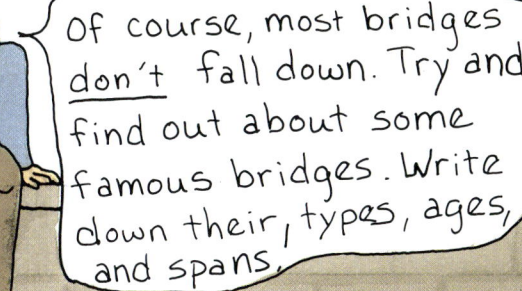

Of course, most bridges don't fall down. Try and find out about some famous bridges. Write down their types, ages, and spans.

♪ San Francisco.. ♪

Sing "London Bridge Is Falling Down" again!

You can now design a strong paper bridge. But would it stand up to the force of a high wind? When designing anything, the engineer needs to know about all the forces at work.

TYPES OF BRIDGES

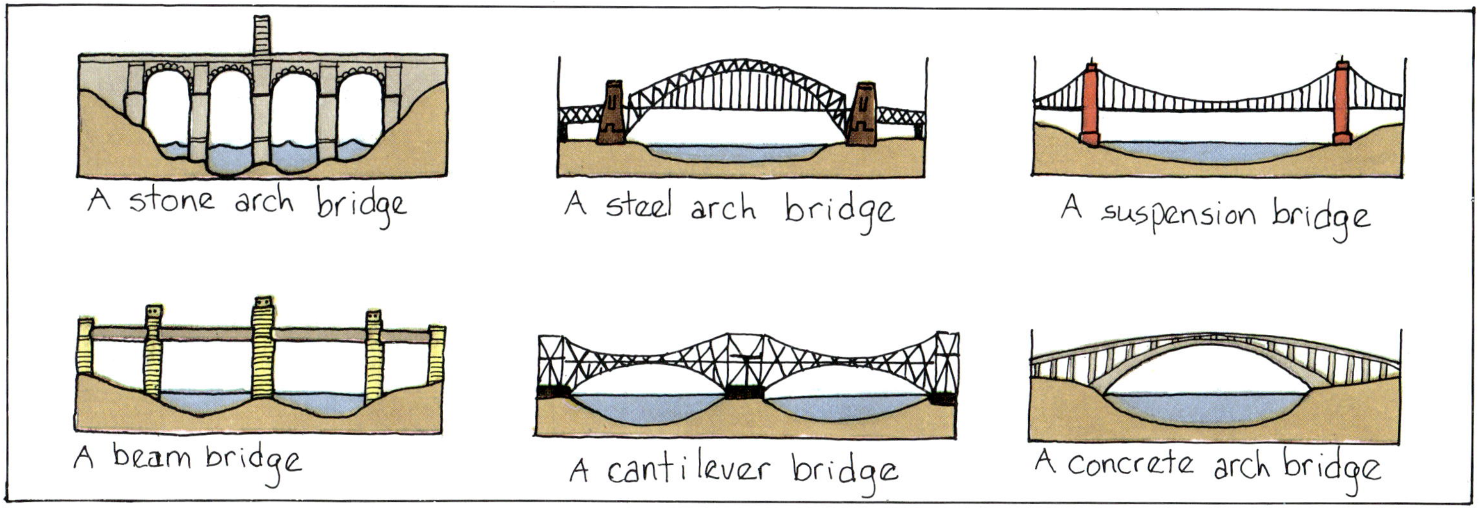

A stone arch bridge

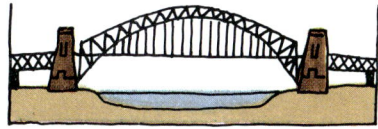

A steel arch bridge

A suspension bridge

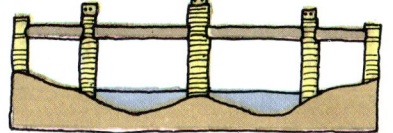

A beam bridge

A cantilever bridge

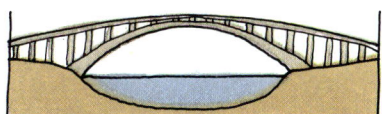

A concrete arch bridge

"Models also play an important role in the development of new aircraft. Every new design is built first as a scale model, then put through a series of tests by engineers."

air disturbance

"One of the tests is to put a model into a wind tunnel. It shows how a full-size plane will behave when it is flying. Instruments inside the model record its performance."

To produce a new airplane, for example, the designer needs to figure out all the forces that will affect the plane as it takes off, flies, and lands. This is very complicated, and the smallest mistake could cause a disaster, if the airplane were built. Today, engineers use computers to help them carry out these calculations so that forces can be balanced to keep the aircraft in the air rather than pull it to the ground.

ZOOM!

PHUT!

"Even if you haven't got a computer, you can still design your own aircraft."

"It can be a simple one, made of balsa wood or paper — or even one with a real engine."

30

Glossary

Atom: the smallest part of an element that can combine with other elements; a source of nuclear energy.
Center of gravity: the point in an object around which its weight is evenly distributed.
Chlorine: a poisonous chemical used to bleach out colors and to purify water by killing germs.
Contract: to get smaller by pulling together; to shrink.
Elastic: able to return to its original shape after being stretched.
Force: the cause that moves an object at rest, or changes the movement of a moving object.
Friction: the resistance to movement of two objects that are touching.
Gravity: the force that draws all objects in the Earth's sphere toward the Earth's center.
Inertia: the tendency of a body to remain as it is, either unmoving or moving at the same rate of speed in the same direction.
Ion: an atom or group of atoms with an electrical charge, positive or negative.
Magnet: a piece of iron or steel that can attract other pieces of iron or steel because of a field of force that surrounds it.
Mass: in physics, a measure of a body's resistance to attraction; mass is proportional to weight and is expressed in kilograms.
Newton: a number that tells how much force it takes to move an object a given distance in a given amount of time.

Index

Airplanes 30
Archimedes 19
Armstrong, Neil 7
Atoms 13, 26-27

Balance 11, 19-20, 21, 30
Bridges 28-29

Center of gravity 20-21
Compass 22

Ear 11-12
Earth 6, 8, 9
Elastic force 15-16, 27
Electric force 23, 24-27

Electromagnetic force 25-27
Electron 26
Electroscope 24

Friction 13-14, 27

Gravity 4-9, 27

Inertia 10-11, 12
Ions 26

Levers 17-19

Magnetic force 22, 24, 25
Mass 5, 6
Mobiles 19
Moon 6-7, 8
Muscles 7, 16-17

Negative charge 25, 26
Newton, Sir Isaac 4, 5, 6
Newtons 5, 6

Pivot 18
Positive charge 25, 26
Proton 26

Semicircular canals 12
Static electricity 23, 24
Strong force 27
Sun 8

Weak force 27
Weight 4, 5, 6, 7
Weightlessness 6, 16

St. James
Catholic School
Montague, Michigan